A+ books

Alphabet Fun

J Is for Jingle Bells

A Christmas Alphabet

by Laura Purdie Salas

CAPSTONE PRESS
a capstone imprint

A is for **anticipation**.

What's inside? Give the gift a little shake.
We're counting down the days until Christmas!

B is for **birthday**.

Christmas is a giant birthday party. On December 25, Christians celebrate the birth of Jesus Christ.

C is for **cookie**.

Santa Claus flies around the world on Christmas Eve to deliver gifts. Do you think he gets tired and hungry? Leave him a snack of milk and cookies.

Santa

D is for **deck the halls**.

Decorating is fun! Tree branches, bows, and ribbons dress up the halls for the holidays.

E is for **elf**.

Santa wouldn't have any presents to deliver without his elves. Santa's helpers work hard building toys at the North Pole.

F is for **family**.

Time spent with family can be the best gift of all. And it doesn't need to be wrapped!

G is for **giving**.

We give gifts to people we love. We also give money and gifts to people in need. Giving helps all families have a happy Christmas.

H is for **holly**.

Holly has been a popular Christmas decoration for hundreds of years. The green leaves and red berries add cheer to the long, cold season.

I is for **ice**.

Did Jack Frost leave ice on your windows? Christmas is cold and snowy for people in northern parts of the world.

J is for jingle bells.

American James Pierpont wrote the song "The One Horse Open Sleigh" in 1857. The song's name was changed to "Jingle Bells" in 1859.

K is for **Kris Kringle**.

Santa Claus is sometimes called Kris Kringle. Kris Kringle probably came from the German name for baby Jesus, *Christkindl*.

L is for **luminaria**.

You can make this easy Mexican decoration. Put some sand in a small paper bag. Place a candle in the sand. Have a grown-up light the candle, and enjoy the glowing show!

13

M is for **music**.

Carolers sing Christmas music as a group. They go door-to-door, singing "Silent Night," "Jingle Bells," and other Christmas songs.

N is for nutcracker.

In *The Nutcracker* ballet, a young girl receives a nutcracker doll for Christmas. The doll comes to life and takes the girl on a magical adventure.

O is for **ornament**.

Shiny balls and sparkling stars.
Bright lights and snowflakes.
They all hang on the tree.

16

P is for **poinsettia**.

Poinsettia plants first grew in Mexico. The colored leaves can be red, white, or pink.

Q is for **quick** and **quiet**.

Santa Claus travels quickly on Christmas Eve to deliver presents. He stays quiet so you don't wake up!

R is for **reindeer**.

Can you name Santa's nine flying reindeer? They are Dasher, Dancer, Prancer, Vixen, Comet, Cupid, Donner, and Blitzen. Wait! Don't forget Rudolph!

S is for **stocking**.

Santa fills your stocking on
Christmas Eve. Good children
get toys. Naughty kids get lumps
of coal. You've been good, right?

T is for **tree**.

The Christmas tree tradition began in Germany long ago. Today real Christmas trees grow outside. Plastic trees can be purchased at a store.

21

U is for **unwrap**.

Christmas has finally arrived. Now it's time to tear off the gift's wrapping paper! Could this be the mermaid doll or the monster truck you asked for?

V is for **visiting Santa**.

Santa and his helpers talk with kids all December. Tell him your Christmas wishes. Then listen for Santa and his reindeer on Christmas Eve.

23

W is for **wreath**.

Make a wreath of evergreen branches, pinecones, and bows. Then hang it on your front door to spread Christmas cheer.

X is for **Xmas**.

People sometimes write "Xmas" instead of "Christmas." That's because Christ is sometimes written as "X." The X is the Greek symbol for the first letter of Christ.

Y is for **yule log**.

People in Europe once burned yule logs during Christmas. They covered the logs with spices and lit them on Christmas Eve. They believed yule logs would bring good luck.

Z is for **dazzle**.

Gaze up at the bright Christmas lights. They sparkle and shine on dark winter nights.

27

Fun Facts about Christmas

 The name Santa Claus came from the Dutch name Sinter Klaas. Santa Claus is also called St. Nicholas, Kris Kringle, and Father Christmas.

 Long ago there was a bishop named St. Nicholas who lived in Turkey. He helped people who were sick or poor. Today many people celebrate St. Nicholas Day each December 6.

 In 1939, Robert L. May wrote a poem called "Rudolph the Red-Nosed Reindeer." The poem was turned into the popular Christmas song in 1949.

 Lighting candles is a Christmas tradition. The shortest day of the year is around December 21. We light candles to celebrate that the days will soon be longer.

 In the southern half of the world, December 25 comes in summer. In Australia, many people go to the beach on Christmas Day. Instead of a hot meal, they might eat cold turkey, ham, or seafood.

 In 1923, U.S. President Calvin Coolidge lit the first National Christmas Tree. It was a Balsam fir that stood 48 feet (14.6 meters) tall.

Glossary

anticipation—the feeling of looking forward to something

ballet—a performance that uses dance to tell a story

bishop—a senior priest in the Catholic church

celebrate—to do something fun on a special day

Christian—a person who follows a religion based on the teachings of Jesus Christ

decoration—an object that makes something prettier or helps it stand out more

holiday—a day to celebrate an event or to honor a person

luminaria—a Mexican Christmas light made of a candle set inside a paper bag

Read More

Butler, Dori Hillestad. *Christmas: Season of Peace and Joy.* Holidays and Culture. Mankato, Minn.: Capstone Press, 2007.

Heiligman, Deborah. *Celebrate Christmas.* Holidays around the World. Washington, D.C.: National Geographic, 2007.

Rustad, Martha E. H. *Christmas in Many Cultures.* Life around the World. Mankato, Minn.: Capstone Press, 2009.

Internet Sites

FactHound offers a safe, fun way to find Internet sites related to this book. All of the sites on FactHound have been researched by our staff.

Here's all you do:

Visit *www.facthound.com*

FactHound will fetch the best sites for you!

Index

A+ Books are published by Capstone Press,
151 Good Counsel Drive, P.O. Box 669, Mankato, Minnesota 56002.
www.capstonepub.com

Copyright © 2011 by Capstone Press, a Capstone imprint.
All rights reserved.
No part of this publication may be reproduced in whole or in part, or stored in a retrieval system,
or transmitted in any form or by any means, electronic, mechanical, photocopying, recording,
or otherwise, without written permission of the publisher.
For information regarding permission, write to Capstone Press,
151 Good Counsel Drive, P.O. Box 669, Dept. R, Mankato, Minnesota 56002.
Printed in the United States of America in North Mankato, Minnesota.
032010
005740CGF10

Library of Congress Cataloging-in-Publication Data
Salas, Laura Purdie.
  J is for jingle bells : a Christmas alphabet / by Laura Purdie Salas.
    p. cm.—(A+ books. Alphabet fun)
  Summary: "Introduces Christmas traditions through photographs and brief text that uses one word relating to the
subject for each letter of the alphabet"—Provided by publisher.
  Includes bibliographical references and index.
  ISBN 978-1-4296-4463-1 (library binding)
  1. Christmas—Juvenile literature. 2. English language—Alphabet—Juvenile literature. I. Title. II. Series.
GT4985.S14 2011
394.2663—dc22   2010001358

Credits
Megan Peterson, editor; Juliette Peters, designer; Laura Manthe, production specialist;
    Sarah Schuette, photo stylist; Marcy Morin, scheduler

Photo Credits
Capstone Studio/Karon Dubke, all photos except:
Alamy/Amoret Tanner: 12, George and Monserrate Schwartz, 10; CORBIS/Tom Bean: 13; Getty Images Inc./
Iconica/Jose Luis Pelaez: 20, Stone/Betsie Van der Meer, 18; iStockphoto/Nicole S. Young: 27

Note to Parents, Teachers, and Librarians
Alphabet Fun books use bold art and photographs and topics with high appeal to engage young children in
learning. Compelling nonfiction content educates and entertains while propelling readers toward mastery of
the alphabet. These books are designed to be read aloud to a pre-reader or read independently by an early
reader. The images help children understand the text and concepts discussed. Alphabet Fun books support
further learning by including the following sections: Fun Facts, Glossary, Read More, Internet Sites, and
Index. Early readers may need assistance using these features.